KITCHEN LIBRARY

Quick & Easy

p

red pepper soup

serves four

225 g/8 oz red peppers, deseeded
    and sliced

1 onion, sliced

2 garlic cloves, crushed

1 fresh green chilli, deseeded
    and chopped

300 ml/10 fl oz passata

600 ml/1 pint vegetable stock

2 tbsp chopped fresh basil

4 fresh basil sprigs, to garnish

VARIATION

This soup is also delicious
served cold with 150 ml/5 fl oz
natural yogurt swirled into it.

1 Put the red peppers into a large pan with the onion, garlic and chilli. Add the passata and stock, then bring to the boil over a medium heat, stirring constantly.

2 Reduce the heat to low and simmer for 20 minutes or until the peppers have softened. Drain, reserving the liquid and vegetables separately.

3 Rub the vegetables through a sieve with the back of a spoon. Alternatively, put into a food processor and process until smooth.

4 Return the purée to a clean pan and add the reserved cooking liquid. Add the chopped basil and heat until hot. Transfer to 4 bowls and garnish with fresh basil sprigs. Serve.

chicken & leek soup

serves six

350 g/12 oz boneless
    chicken breasts
350 g/12 oz leeks
25 g/1 oz butter
1.2 litres/2 pints chicken stock
1 bouquet garni
8 stoned prunes
cooked rice and diced
    peppers, optional
salt and white pepper

VARIATION

Instead of a bouquet garni
sachet, you can use a bunch of
fresh mixed herbs, tied together
with string. Choose herbs such as
parsley, thyme and rosemary.

1 Using a sharp knife, cut the
chicken and leeks into 2.5-cm/
1-inch pieces.

2 Melt the butter in a large pan
over a medium heat. Add the
chicken and leeks and sauté for
8 minutes, stirring occasionally.

3 Add the stock and bouquet garni
to the mixture in the pan. Season
to taste with salt and white pepper.

4 Bring the soup to the boil over a
medium heat, then reduce the
heat and simmer for 45 minutes.

5 Add the stoned prunes with some
cooked rice and diced peppers
(if using) and simmer for 20 minutes.
Remove the bouquet garni and
discard. Ladle the soup into a warmed
tureen or serving bowls and serve.

pumpkin soup

serves four

2 tbsp olive oil

2 medium onions, chopped

2 garlic cloves, chopped

900 g/2 lb pumpkin, peeled and cut
into 2.5-cm/1-inch chunks

1.5 litres/2¾ pints boiling vegetable
or chicken stock

finely grated rind and juice of
1 orange

3 tbsp fresh thyme leaves

150 ml/5 fl oz milk

salt and pepper

crusty bread, to serve

COOK'S TIP

Pumpkins are usually
large vegetables. To make
things a little easier, ask the
greengrocer to cut a chunk off
for you. Alternatively, make
double the quantity and freeze
the soup for up to 3 months.

---

1 Heat the oil in a large frying pan over a medium heat. Add the onions and cook, stirring occasionally, for 3–4 minutes until softened. Add the garlic and pumpkin and cook, stirring, for a further 2 minutes.

2 Add the boiling stock, orange rind and juice and 2 tablespoons of the fresh thyme to the pan. Cover and simmer for 20 minutes, or until the pumpkin is tender.

3 Transfer the mixture to a food processor and process until smooth. Alternatively, put the mixture into a bowl and mash with a potato masher until smooth. Season to taste with salt and pepper.

4 Return the soup to the pan and add the milk. Heat gently for about 3–4 minutes, or until hot.

5 Sprinkle with the remaining fresh thyme just before serving.

6 Ladle the soup into 4 warmed soup bowls and serve with lots of fresh, crusty bread.

spicy dhal & carrot soup

serves six

125 g/4½ oz split red lentils

1.2 litres/2 pints vegetable stock

350 g/12 oz carrots, sliced

2 onions, chopped

225 g/8 oz canned
    chopped tomatoes

2 garlic cloves, chopped

2 tbsp ghee or vegetable oil

1 tsp ground cumin

1 tsp ground coriander

1 fresh green chilli, deseeded
    and chopped

½ tsp turmeric

1 tbsp lemon juice

300 ml/10 fl oz milk

2 tbsp chopped fresh coriander

salt

natural yogurt, to serve

COOK'S TIP

Lentils play an important part in ensuring that a healthy diet is maintained and provide energy-rich carbohydrates. Current guidelines recommend that 50% of our daily energy requirements come from carbohydrates.

1 Put the lentils into a sieve and rinse well under cold running water. Drain and put into a large pan, together with 850 ml/1½ pints of the stock, the carrots, onions, tomatoes and garlic. Bring to the boil over a medium heat, then cover and simmer for 30 minutes, or until the vegetables and lentils are tender.

2 Meanwhile, heat the ghee in a small pan over a low heat. Add the cumin, ground coriander, chilli and turmeric and fry for 1 minute. Remove from the heat and stir in the lemon juice. Season with salt to taste.

3 Working in batches, transfer the soup to a food processor and process until smooth. Return to the pan, add the spice mixture and remaining 300 ml/10 fl oz of stock and cook over a low heat for 10 minutes.

4 Add the milk, taste and adjust the seasoning, if necessary. Stir in the chopped coriander and heat through. Ladle the soup into 6 warmed bowls and serve hot with a swirl of yogurt.

fresh mushroom soup

serves four

40 g/1½ oz butter

700 g/1 lb 9 oz mushrooms, sliced

1 onion, chopped finely

1 shallot, chopped finely

25 g/1 oz plain flour

2–3 tbsp dry white wine or sherry

l.4 litres/2½ pints vegetable stock

150 ml/5 fl oz single cream

2 tbsp chopped fresh parsley

fresh lemon juice, optional

salt and pepper

TO GARNISH

4 tbsp soured cream

4 fresh herb sprigs

1 Melt half the butter in a frying pan over a low heat. Add the mushrooms and season with salt and pepper. Cook for 8 minutes, or until golden, stirring occasionally at first, then more often after they start to colour. Remove from the heat.

2 Melt the remaining butter in a pan over a low heat. Add the onion and shallot and fry until softened Stir in the flour and cook for 2 minutes, then stir in the wine and stock.

3 Reserve about one-quarter of the mushrooms and add the remainder to the pan. Reduce the heat, cover and cook gently for 20 minutes, stirring occasionally.

4 Leave to cool, then working in batches, transfer the soup to a food processor or blender and process until a smooth purée forms. (If using a food processor, strain off the liquid and reserve. Purée the solids with enough cooking liquid to moisten them, then mix with the remaining liquid.)

5 Return the soup to the pan and stir in the reserved mushrooms, the cream and parsley. Cook for about 5 minutes to heat through. Taste and adjust the seasoning, adding a little lemon juice, if you wish. Ladle the soup into 4 bowls, garnish with soured cream and fresh herb sprigs. Serve.

spinach & mascarpone soup

serves four

55 g/2 oz butter

1 bunch spring onions, chopped

2 celery sticks, chopped

350 g/12 oz spinach or sorrel, or
3 bunches watercress

850 ml/1½ pints vegetable stock

225 g/8 oz mascarpone cheese

1 tbsp olive oil

2 slices thick-cut bread, cut
into cubes

½ tsp caraway seeds

salt and pepper

sesame breadsticks, to serve

1 Melt half the butter in a very large pan over a medium heat. Add the spring onions and celery, and cook, stirring frequently, for about 5 minutes, or until softened.

2 Pack the spinach, sorrel or watercress into the pan. Add the stock and bring to the boil over a medium heat, then reduce the heat, cover and simmer for 15–20 minutes.

3 Transfer the soup to a food processor or blender and process until smooth. Alternatively, rub through a sieve with the back of a spoon, then return to the pan.

4 Add the mascarpone cheese to the soup and heat gently, stirring constantly, until smooth and blended. Season to taste with salt and pepper.

5 Heat the remaining butter with the oil in a frying pan over a medium heat. Add the bread cubes and fry, turning frequently, until golden brown. Add the caraway seeds towards the end of cooking to prevent them burning.

6 Ladle the soup into 4 warmed bowls. Sprinkle with the croûtons and serve with sesame breadsticks.

hummus & garlic toasts

serves four

400 g/14 oz canned chick-peas

juice of 1 large lemon

6 tbsp tahini

2 tbsp olive oil

2 garlic cloves, crushed

salt and pepper

GARLIC TOASTS

1 ciabatta loaf, sliced

2 garlic cloves, crushed

1 tbsp chopped fresh coriander

4 tbsp olive oil

TO GARNISH

1 tbsp chopped fresh coriander

6 stoned black olives

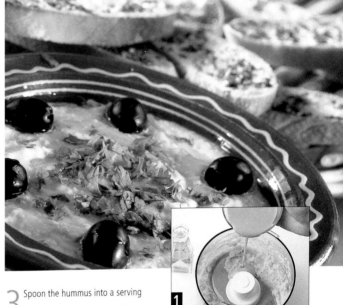

1 To make the hummus, firstly drain the chick-peas, reserving about 2–3 tablespoons of the liquid. Put the chick-peas and half the liquid into a food processor and blend, gradually adding the remaining liquid and lemon juice. Blend well after each addition until smooth.

2 Stir in the tahini and all but 1 teaspoon of the oil. Add the garlic, season to taste with salt and pepper and blend again until smooth.

3 Spoon the hummus into a serving dish. Drizzle the remaining oil over the top and chill in the refrigerator.

4 To make the garlic toasts, lay the slices of ciabatta on a grill rack in a single layer.

5 Mix the garlic, coriander and oil together and drizzle over the bread. Cook under a preheated medium-hot grill for 2–3 minutes until golden, turning once. To serve, garnish the hummus with chopped coriander and olives, then serve with the toasts.

cheese & onion röstis

serves four

900 g/2 lb potatoes

1 onion, grated

50 g/1¼ oz Gruyère cheese, grated

2 tbsp chopped fresh parsley

1 tbsp olive oil

2 tbsp butter

salt and pepper

TO GARNISH

1 spring onion, shredded

1 small tomato, quartered

1 Parboil the potatoes in a pan of lightly salted, boiling water for 10 minutes and leave to cool. Peel the potatoes and grate with a coarse grater. Place the grated potatoes in a large mixing bowl.

2 Stir in the onion, cheese and parsley. Season well with salt and pepper. Divide the potato mixture into 4 portions of equal size and form them into cakes.

3 Heat half of the olive oil with half the butter in a frying pan and cook 2 of the potato cakes over a high heat for 1 minute, then reduce the heat and cook for 5 minutes, until they are golden underneath. Turn them over and cook for a further 5 minutes.

4 Repeat with the other half of the olive oil and the remaining butter to cook the remaining 2 potato cakes. Transfer the röstis to warm individual serving plates, garnish with shredded spring onion and tomato quarters and serve immediately.

COOK'S TIP

The potato cakes should be flattened as much as possible during cooking, otherwise the outsides will be cooked before the centres are done.

pepper salad

serves four

1 onion

2 red peppers

2 yellow peppers

3 tbsp olive oil

2 large courgettes, sliced

2 garlic cloves, sliced

1 tbsp balsamic vinegar

50 g/1¾ oz canned anchovy fillets,
    drained and chopped

25 g/1 oz stoned black
    olives, halved

salt and pepper

4 fresh basil sprigs, to garnish

TOMATO TOASTS

1 small French bread stick

1 garlic clove, crushed

1 fresh tomato, peeled and chopped

2 tbsp olive oil

1 Cut the onion into wedges. Core and deseed the peppers, then cut into thick slices.

2 Heat the oil in a large heavy-based frying pan over a low heat. Add the onion, peppers, courgettes and garlic and fry for 20 minutes, stirring occasionally.

3 Add the vinegar, anchovies and olives. Season to taste with salt and pepper. Mix and leave to cool.

4 To make the tomato toasts, cut the French bread diagonally into 1-cm/½-inch slices.

5 Mix the garlic, tomato and oil together. Season to taste and spread thinly over each slice of bread.

6 Put the bread on to a baking tray, drizzle with the oil and bake in a preheated oven at 220°C/425°F/Gas Mark 7, for 5–10 minutes until crisp. Spoon the salad on to 4 individual plates, garnish with basil sprigs and serve with the tomato toasts.

bruschetta with tomatoes

serves four

300 g/10½ oz cherry tomatoes

4 sun-dried tomatoes

4 tbsp extra virgin olive oil

16 fresh basil leaves

8 slices of ciabatta bread

2 garlic cloves, peeled

salt and pepper

VARIATION

Plum tomatoes are also good in this recipe. Halve them, then cut them into wedges. Mix them with the sun-dried tomatoes in step 3.

COOK'S TIP

Ciabatta is an Italian rustic bread, which is slightly holey and quite chewy. It is very good in this recipe as it absorbs the full flavour of the garlic and extra virgin olive oil.

1 Cut the cherry tomatoes in half with a sharp knife.

2 Slice the sun-dried tomatoes into strips with a sharp knife.

3 Put the cherry tomatoes and sun-dried tomatoes into a small bowl. Add the oil and the basil leaves and, using a spoon, toss to mix well. Season to taste with salt and pepper.

4 Lightly toast the ciabatta slices under a preheated medium-hot grill. Cut the garlic cloves in half.

5 Rub the garlic, cut-side down, over both sides of the toasted ciabatta slices.

6 Put the ciabatta on to a serving plate or individual plates and top with the tomato mixture. Serve.

capri salad

serves four

2 beef tomatoes

125 g/4½ oz mozzarella cheese

12 black olives

8 fresh basil leaves

1 tbsp balsamic vinegar

1 tbsp extra virgin olive oil

salt and pepper

fresh basil leaves, to garnish

COOK'S TIP

Buffalo mozzarella cheese, although it is usually more expensive because of the comparative rarity of buffalo, does have a better flavour than the cow's milk variety. It is popular in salads, but also provides a tangy layer in baked dishes.

1 Cut the tomatoes into thin slices with a sharp knife.

2 Drain the mozzarella cheese, if necessary, and cut into thin slices with a sharp knife.

3 Stone the black olives, if necessary and slice into rings.

4 Layer the tomatoes, mozzarella cheese slices, olives and basil leaves in a stack, finishing with a layer of mozzarella cheese on top.

5 Put each stack under a preheated hot grill for 2–3 minutes, or just long enough to melt the mozzarella.

6 Drizzle over the balsamic vinegar and oil and season to taste with a little salt and pepper.

7 Transfer to 4 large serving plates and garnish with a few fresh basil leaves. Serve immediately.

tuna, bean & anchovy salad

serves four

500 g/1 lb 2 oz tomatoes

200 g/7 oz canned tuna, drained

2 tbsp chopped fresh parsley

½ cucumber

1 small red onion

225 g/8 oz cooked green beans

1 small red pepper, deseeded

1 small crisp lettuce

6 tbsp Italian-style dressing

3 hard-boiled eggs

55 g/2 oz canned anchovy
  fillets, drained

12 stoned black olives

1 Cut the tomatoes into wedges, flake the tuna and put both into a large bowl with the chopped parsley.

2 Cut the cucumber into slices. Slice the onion. Add the cucumber and onion to the bowl.

3 Cut the green beans in half, chop the pepper and add both to the bowl with the lettuce. Pour over the dressing and toss to mix well, then spoon into a salad bowl. Shell the eggs and cut into quarters. Add to the salad with the anchovies, then scatter over the olives and serve.

smoked trout & apple salad

serves four

2 orange-red eating apples

2 tbsp French dressing

½ bunch watercress

1 smoked trout, about 175 g/6 oz

Melba Toast, to serve (see

   Cook's Tip)

HORSERADISH DRESSING

125 ml/4 fl oz low-fat natural yogurt

½–1 tsp lemon juice

1 tbsp horseradish sauce

milk, optional

salt and pepper

TO GARNISH

1 tbsp snipped fresh chives

fresh chive flowers, optional

COOK'S TIP

To make the Melba Toast, toast
medium sliced bread, then cut off
the crusts and carefully slice in
half horizontally using a sharp
knife. Cut in half diagonally
and put toasted side down in a
warmed oven for 15–20 minutes
until the edges start to curl and
the toast is crisp.

1 Leaving the skin on, cut the apples into quarters and remove the cores. Slice the apples into a bowl and toss in the French dressing to prevent them turning brown.

2 Break the watercress into sprigs and arrange on 4 serving plates.

3 Skin the trout and take out the bone. Carefully remove any fine bones that remain, using your fingers or tweezers. Flake the trout into fairly large pieces and arrange with the apple between the watercress.

4 To make the horseradish dressing, whisk all the ingredients together, adding a little milk if too thick, then drizzle over the trout. Sprinkle the snipped chives and flowers (if using) over the trout and serve with Melba Toast (see Cook's Tip).

neapolitan seafood salad

serves four

450 g/1 lb prepared squid, cut
  into strips
750 g/1 lb 10 oz cooked mussels
450 g/1 lb cooked cockles in brine
150 ml/5 fl oz white wine
300 ml/10 fl oz olive oil
225 g/8 oz dried campanelle
  or other small pasta shapes
juice of 1 lemon
1 bunch fresh chives, snipped
1 bunch fresh parsley,
  chopped finely
4 large tomatoes
mixed salad leaves
salt and pepper
1 fresh basil sprig, to garnish

1 Put the seafood into a large bowl, pour over the wine and half the oil. Cover, then chill for 6 hours.

2 Put the mixture into a pan and simmer over a low heat for 10 minutes. Remove and leave to cool.

3 Bring a pan of lightly salted water to the boil over a medium heat. Add the pasta and 1 tablespoon of the remaining oil and cook until tender, but still firm to the bite.

4 Strain off about half of the cooking liquid from the seafood and reserve. Discard the rest. Mix in the lemon juice, herbs and remaining oil. Season to taste with salt and pepper. Drain the pasta and add to the seafood.

5 Cut the tomatoes into quarters. Shred the salad leaves and arrange them at the base of a salad bowl. Spoon in the seafood salad and garnish with the quartered tomatoes and a fresh basil sprig. Serve.

smoky fish skewers

serves four

350 g/12 oz smoked cod fillet

350 g/12 oz cod fillet

8 large raw prawns

8 bay leaves

fresh dill sprigs, to garnish (optional)

MARINADE

4 tbsp sunflower oil, plus a little
    for brushing

2 tbsp lemon or lime juice

grated rind of ½ lemon or lime

¼ tsp dried dill

salt and pepper

1 Skin both types of cod and cut the flesh into bite-sized pieces. Peel the prawns, leaving just the tail.

2 To make the marinade, mix the oil, lemon juice and rind, dried dill and seasoning to taste together in a shallow, non-metallic dish.

3 Put the fish in the marinade and stir well. Leave to marinate in the refrigerator for 1–4 hours.

4 Thread the fish on to 4 metal skewers, alternating the fish with the prawns and bay leaves.

5 Cover a barbecue rack with lightly oiled tinfoil. Put the skewers on top and cook over a medium-hot barbecue for 5–10 minutes, basting with marinade. Turn once. Transfer the skewers to a warmed serving platter, garnish with fresh dill, if you wish and serve.

poached salmon with penne

serves four

4 x 280 g/10 oz fresh salmon steaks

55 g/2 oz butter

175 ml/6 fl oz dry white wine

pinch of sea salt

8 peppercorns

1 fresh dill sprig

1 fresh tarragon sprig

1 lemon, sliced

450 g/1 lb dried penne

1 tbsp olive oil

SAUCE

25 g/1 oz butter

25 g/1 oz plain flour

150 ml/5 fl oz warm milk

juice and grated rind of 2 lemons

55 g/2 oz watercress, chopped

salt and pepper

TO GARNISH

lemon slices

fresh watercress

1 Put the salmon into a large frying pan. Add the butter, wine, sea salt, peppercorns, dill, tarragon and lemon. Cover, bring to the boil over a low heat and simmer for 10 minutes.

2 Carefully remove the salmon with a fish slice. Strain and reserve the cooking liquid. Remove the salmon skin and centre bones and discard. Put into a dish, cover and keep warm.

3 Meanwhile, bring a large pan of lightly salted water to the boil over a medium heat. Add the pasta and 1 teaspoon of the oil and cook for 12 minutes, or until tender, but still firm to the bite. Drain and sprinkle over the remaining oil. Put into a warmed serving dish, top with the salmon steaks and keep warm.

4 To make the sauce, melt the butter over a low heat and stir in the flour for 2 minutes. Stir in the milk and 7 tablespoons of the cooking liquid. Add the lemon juice and rind and cook, stirring, for 10 minutes.

5 Add the watercress to the sauce, stir gently and season to taste with salt and pepper.

6 Pour the sauce over the salmon, garnish with lemon slices and watercress and serve immediately.

rice with crab & mussels

serves four

300 g/10½ oz long-grain rice

175 g/6 oz white crabmeat, fresh,
    canned or frozen (thawed if
    frozen), or 8 crab sticks,
    thawed if frozen

2 tbsp sesame or sunflower oil

2.5-cm/1-inch piece fresh root
    ginger, grated

4 spring onions, thinly sliced
    diagonally

125 g/4½ oz mangetout, cut into
    2–3 pieces

½ tsp turmeric

1 tsp ground cumin

400 g/14 oz bottled mussels, well
    drained, or 350 g/12 oz frozen
    mussels, thawed

425 g/15 oz canned bean sprouts,
    well drained

salt and pepper

1 Bring a pan of lightly salted water to the boil over a medium heat. Add the rice and cook for 15 minutes. Drain and keep warm.

2 Extract the crabmeat, if using fresh crab. Flake the crabmeat or cut the crab sticks into 3–4 pieces.

3 Heat a large wok over a high heat. Add the oil and when hot, add the ginger and spring onions. Stir-fry for 1–2 minutes. Add the mangetout and continue to cook for a further minute. Sprinkle the turmeric and cumin over the vegetables, then season to taste with salt and pepper. Mix thoroughly.

4 Add the crabmeat or crab sticks and mussels and stir-fry for 1 minute. Stir in the cooked rice and bean sprouts and stir-fry for a further 2 minutes, or until hot and well mixed.

5 Adjust the seasoning to taste, if necessary. Transfer to a large serving dish and serve immediately.

seafood chow mein

serves four

90 g/3¼ oz squid, cleaned

3–4 fresh scallops

90 g/3¼ oz raw prawns, peeled

½ egg white, beaten lightly

1 tbsp cornflour paste (see

    Cook's Tip)

280 g/10 oz dried egg noodles

5–6 tbsp vegetable oil

2 tbsp light soy sauce

55 g/2 oz mangetout

½ tsp salt

½ tsp sugar

1 tsp Chinese rice wine

2 spring onions,

    shredded finely

few drops of sesame oil

1 Open up the squid and score the inside in a criss-cross pattern, then cut into pieces about the size of a postage stamp. Soak the squid in a bowl of boiling water until all the pieces curl up. Rinse in cold water and drain.

2 Cut each scallop into 3–4 slices. Cut the prawns in half lengthways, if large. Mix the scallops and prawns together with the egg white and cornflour paste.

3 Bring a large pan of water to the boil over a medium heat. Add the noodles and cook for 5–6 minutes. Drain and rinse under cold running water and drain well. Toss with about 1 tablespoon of the oil.

4 Heat a wok over a high heat. Add 3 tablespoons of oil and when hot, add the noodles and 1 tablespoon of the soy sauce. Stir-fry for about 2–3 minutes. Transfer to a serving dish.

5 Heat the remaining oil in the wok and add the mangetout and seafood. Stir-fry for 2 minutes, then add the salt, sugar, Chinese rice wine, remaining soy sauce and about half the spring onions. Blend well and add a little water, if necessary. Pour the mixture on top of the noodles and sprinkle with sesame oil. Garnish with the remaining spring onions and serve.

COOK'S TIP

Cornflour paste is made by mixing 1 part cornflour with about 1½ parts of cold water. Stir until smooth

noodles with prawns

serves four

225 g/8 oz thin egg noodles

2 tbsp peanut oil

1 garlic clove, crushed

½ tsp ground star anise

1 bunch spring onions, cut into
    5-cm/2-inch pieces

24 raw tiger prawns, peeled with
    tails intact

2 tbsp light soy sauce

2 tsp lime juice

slices of lime, to garnish

COOK'S TIP

If fresh egg noodles are
available, these require very little
cooking. Simply put into boiling
water for about 3 minutes, then
drain and toss in oil. Noodles can
be boiled and eaten plain, or stir-
fried with meat and vegetables
for a light meal or snack.

1 Bring a pan of water to the boil over a medium heat. Add the noodles and blanch for 2 minutes.

2 Drain the noodles well, rinse under cold running water and drain thoroughly again. Keep warm and reserve until required.

3 Heat a large wok over a high heat. Add the peanut oil and when almost smoking, add the garlic and ground star anise and stir-fry for 30 seconds.

4 Add the spring onions and tiger prawns to the wok and stir-fry for 2–3 minutes.

5 Stir in the soy sauce, lime juice and noodles and mix well.

6 Cook the mixture in the wok for about 1 minute, or until heated through and all the ingredients are incorporated.

7 Transfer the noodle and prawn mixture to 4 warmed serving bowls and garnish with slices of lime. Serve immediately.

scallop skewers

serves four

grated zest and juice of 2 limes

2 tbsp finely chopped lemon grass
    or 1 tbsp lemon juice

2 garlic cloves, crushed

1 fresh green chilli, deseeded
    and chopped

16 scallops, with corals

2 limes, each cut into 8 segments

2 tbsp sunflower oil

1 tbsp lemon juice

salt and pepper

TO SERVE

55 g/2 oz rocket

200 g/7 oz mixed salad leaves

1 Soak 8 wooden skewers in warm water for at least 30 minutes before you use them to prevent the skewers burning on the barbecue.

2 Mix the lime juice and zest, lemon grass, garlic and chilli together in a mortar with a pestle to make a paste. Alternatively, use a spice grinder.

3 Thread 2 scallops on to each of the presoaked skewers. Cover the ends with a piece of tinfoil to prevent them burning.

4 Alternate the scallops with the lime segments.

5 Put the oil, lemon juice, salt and pepper into a small bowl and whisk together to make a dressing.

6 Coat the scallops with the prepared spice paste and put over a medium-hot barbecue.

7 Cook the scallops for 10 minutes, basting occasionally. Turn once.

8 Toss the rocket, mixed salad leaves and dressing together well. Transfer to a large serving bowl.

9 Serve the scallops piping hot, 2 skewers on each plate immediately, with the salad.

spaghetti & salmon sauce

serves four

500 g/1 lb 2 oz dried
   buckwheat spaghetti

2 tbsp olive oil

85 g/3 oz feta cheese, crumbled
   (drained weight)

1 tbsp chopped fresh coriander or
   parsley, to garnish

SALMON SAUCE

300 ml/10 fl oz double cream

150 ml/5 fl oz whisky or brandy

125 g/4½ oz smoked salmon

large pinch of cayenne pepper

2 tbsp chopped fresh coriander
   or parsley

salt and pepper

1 Bring a large pan of lightly salted water to the boil over a medium heat. Add the pasta and cook for about 8–10 minutes, or until tender, but still firm to the bite. Drain thoroughly and return to the pan, sprinkle over the oil, cover the pan and shake well. Reserve and keep warm until required.

2 To make the sauce, heat the cream and the whisky or brandy in separate small pans to simmering point. Do not let them boil.

3 Mix the cream with the whisky or brandy in a bowl.

4 Cut the smoked salmon into thin strips and add to the cream mixture. Season to taste with a little pepper and cayenne pepper, then stir in the chopped coriander or parsley.

5 Transfer the pasta to a large, warmed serving dish, pour on the sauce and toss thoroughly, using 2 large forks. Scatter the crumbled feta cheese over the pasta and garnish with chopped coriander. Serve immediately.

lamb with olives

serves four

1.25 kg/2 lb 12 oz boned leg
of lamb

6 tbsp olive oil

2 garlic cloves, crushed

1 onion, sliced

1 small fresh red chilli, deseeded
and chopped finely

175 ml/6 fl oz dry white wine

175 g/6 oz stoned black olives

salt

1 fresh flat-leaf parsley sprig,
to garnish

1 Cut the lamb into 2.5-cm/1-inch cubes with a sharp knife.

2 Heat the oil in a frying pan over a medium heat. Add the garlic, onion and chilli and fry for 5 minutes.

3 Add the meat and wine and cook for a further 5 minutes.

4 Stir in the olives, then transfer the mixture to a casserole dish. Cook in a preheated oven at 180°C/350°F/ Gas Mark 4, for 1 hour 20 minutes, or until the meat is tender. Season with salt to taste. Transfer to a serving plate, garnish with a parsley sprig and serve.

lamb cutlets with rosemary

serves four

8 lamb cutlets

5 tbsp olive oil

2 tbsp lemon juice

1 garlic clove, crushed

½ tsp lemon pepper

salt

8 fresh rosemary sprigs

baked jacket potatoes, to serve

SALAD

4 tomatoes, sliced

4 spring onions, sliced diagonally

DRESSING

2 tbsp olive oil

1 tbsp lemon juice

1 garlic clove, chopped

¼ tsp chopped fresh rosemary

1 Trim the lamb cutlets by cutting away the flesh with a sharp knife to expose the tips of the bones.

2 Put the oil, lemon juice, garlic, lemon pepper and salt into a non-metallic dish and mix with a fork.

3 Lay the rosemary sprigs in the dish and put the lamb on top. Leave to marinate in the refrigerator for at least 1 hour, turning the lamb once.

4 Remove the lamb from the marinade and wrap tinfoil around the bones to stop them burning.

5 Put the rosemary sprigs on the barbecue rack and put the lamb on top. Cook on a hot barbecue for 10–15 minutes, turning once.

6 Meanwhile, make the salad and dressing. Arrange the tomatoes on a serving dish and scatter the spring onions on top. Put all the ingredients for the dressing in a screw-top jar, shake well and pour over the salad. Serve with the barbecued lamb cutlets and baked jacket potatoes.

rich chicken casserole

serves four

8 chicken thighs

2 tbsp olive oil

1 medium red onion, sliced

2 garlic cloves, crushed

1 large red pepper, sliced thickly

thinly pared rind and juice of

    1 small orange

125 ml/4 fl oz chicken stock

400 g/14 oz canned

    chopped tomatoes

25 g/1 oz sun-dried tomatoes,

    sliced thinly

1 tbsp chopped fresh thyme

50 g/1¾ oz stoned black olives

salt and pepper

crusty bread, to serve

TO GARNISH

orange rind

4 fresh thyme sprigs

COOK'S TIP

Sun-dried tomatoes have a dense
texture and concentrated taste
and add intense flavour to
slow-cooking casseroles.

1 In a large heavy-based frying pan, fry the chicken without fat over a fairly high heat, turning occasionally, until golden brown. Drain off any excess fat from the chicken with a slotted spoon and transfer to a flameproof casserole dish.

2 Heat the oil in the frying pan over a medium heat. Add the onion, garlic and red pepper and fry for about 3–4 minutes. Transfer the vegetables to the casserole dish.

3 Add the orange rind and juice, stock, chopped tomatoes and sun-dried tomatoes to the casserole and mix well.

4 Bring to the boil, then cover the casserole with a lid and simmer very gently over a low heat for about 1 hour, stirring occasionally. Add the chopped thyme and black olives, then season to taste with salt and pepper.

5 Spoon the chicken casserole on to 4 warmed serving plates, garnish with orange rind and thyme sprigs and serve with crusty bread.

garlic & herb chicken

serves four

4 chicken breasts, skin removed

100 g/3½ oz full-fat soft cheese, flavoured with herbs and garlic

8 slices Parma ham

150 ml/5 fl oz red wine

150 ml/5 fl oz chicken stock

1 tbsp brown sugar

green salad leaves, to serve

1 Using a sharp knife, make a horizontal slit along the length of each chicken breast to form a pocket.

2 Put the cheese into a bowl and beat thoroughly with a wooden spoon to soften it. Spoon the cheese into the pocket of the chicken breasts.

3 Wrap 2 slices of Parma ham around each chicken breast and secure with a length of string.

4 Pour the wine and stock in a large frying pan and bring to the boil over a medium heat. When the mixture is just starting to boil, add the sugar and stir to dissolve.

5 Add the chicken breasts to the mixture in the pan. Simmer for 12–15 minutes, or until the chicken is tender and the juices run clear when a skewer is inserted into the thickest part of the meat.

6 Remove the chicken from the pan, reserve and keep warm.

7 Heat the sauce and boil until reduced and thickened. Remove the string from the chicken and cut into slices. Pour the sauce over the chicken and serve with salad leaves.

VARIATION

Try adding 2 finely chopped sun-dried tomatoes to the soft cheese in step 2, if you wish.

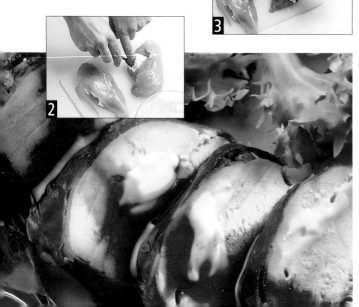

chicken pepperonata

serves four

8 skinless chicken thighs

2 tbsp wholemeal flour

2 tbsp olive oil

1 small onion, sliced thinly

1 garlic clove, crushed

1 each large red, yellow and green
    peppers, sliced thinly

400 g/14 oz canned
    chopped tomatoes

1 tbsp chopped fresh oregano

salt and pepper

fresh oregano leaves, to garnish

COOK'S TIP

If you do not have fresh oregano,
use canned tomatoes with herbs
already added.

1 Skin the chicken thighs and toss
in the flour.

2 Heat the oil in a frying pan over a
high heat. Add the chicken and
fry until browned. Remove from the
pan. Add the onion and fry until soft.
Add the garlic, peppers, tomatoes and
oregano. Bring to the boil, stirring.

3 Arrange the chicken over the
vegetables. Season well with salt
and pepper, then cover the pan tightly
and simmer for 20–25 minutes, or until
the chicken is tender and the juices run
clear when a skewer is inserted into
the thickest part of the meat.

4 Season to taste, then transfer the
chicken to a large serving dish,
garnish with oregano leaves and serve.

39

mustard-baked chicken

serves four

4 large or 8 small chicken pieces

4 tbsp butter, melted

4 tbsp mild mustard (see Cook's Tip)

2 tbsp lemon juice

1 tbsp brown sugar

1 tsp paprika

3 tbsp poppy seeds

400 g/14 oz dried pasta shells

1 tbsp olive oil

salt and pepper

COOK'S TIP

Dijon is the type of mustard most often used in cooking, as it has a clean and only mildly spicy flavour. German mustard has a sweet-sour taste, with Bavarian mustard being slightly sweeter. American mustard is mild and sweet.

1 Arrange all the chicken pieces in a single layer in a large oven-proof dish.

2 Mix the butter, mustard, lemon juice, sugar and paprika together in a small bowl and season to taste with salt and pepper. Brush the mixture over the upper surfaces of the chicken pieces and bake in a preheated oven at 200°C/400°F/Gas Mark 6, for about 15 minutes.

3 Remove the dish from the oven and carefully turn the chicken pieces over with tongs. Coat the upper surfaces of the chicken with the remaining mustard mixture, then sprinkle the chicken pieces with poppy seeds. Return to the oven for a further 15 minutes.

4 Meanwhile, bring a large pan of lightly salted water to the boil over a medium heat. Add the pasta shells and oil and cook for about 8–10 minutes, or until tender, but still firm to the bite.

5 Drain the pasta thoroughly and transfer to 4 warmed serving plates. Top the pasta with 1 or 2 of the chicken pieces, pour over the sauce and serve immediately.

chicken with green olives

serves four

3 tbsp olive oil

2 tbsp butter

4 part boned chicken breasts

1 large onion, chopped finely

2 garlic cloves, crushed

2 red, yellow or green peppers,
    deseeded and cut into pieces

250 g/9 oz button mushrooms,
    sliced or quartered

175 g/6 oz tomatoes, peeled
    and halved

150 ml/5 fl oz dry white wine

175 g/6 oz stoned green olives

4–6 tbsp double cream

400 g/14 oz dried pasta

salt and pepper

chopped fresh flat-leaf parsley,
    to garnish

1 Heat all but 1 teaspoon of the oil and the butter in a frying pan over a medium heat. Add the chicken breasts and fry until golden brown. Remove the chicken from the pan.

2 Add the onion and garlic to the pan and fry over a medium heat until starting to soften. Add the peppers and mushrooms and cook for 2–3 minutes.

3 Add the tomatoes and season to taste with salt and pepper. Transfer the vegetables to a casserole dish and arrange the chicken on top.

4 Add the wine to the pan and bring to the boil over a medium heat. Pour the wine over the chicken. Cover and cook the casserole in a preheated oven at 180°C/350°F/ Gas Mark 4, for 50 minutes.

5 Add the olives to the casserole and mix in. Pour in the cream, cover and return to the oven for a further 10–20 minutes.

6 Meanwhile, bring a large pan of lightly salted water to the boil over a medium heat. Add the pasta and remaining oil and cook for 8–10 minutes, or until tender, but still firm to the bite. Drain well and transfer to a warmed serving dish.

7 Serve the chicken straight from the casserole dish, garnished with chopped parsley with the pasta served separately. Alternatively, arrange the chicken on top of the pasta, spoon over the sauce, garnish with chopped parsley and serve immediately.

pork chops with sage

serves four

2 tbsp flour

1 tbsp chopped fresh sage or
    1 tsp dried sage

4 boneless, lean pork chops,
    trimmed of excess fat

2 tbsp olive oil

15 g/½ oz butter

2 red onions, sliced into rings

1 tbsp lemon juice

2 tsp caster sugar

4 plum tomatoes, quartered

salt and pepper

green salad, to serve

1 Mix the flour, sage and salt and pepper to taste on a large plate. Lightly dust the pork chops on both sides with the seasoned flour.

2 Heat 2 tablespoons of the oil and butter in a large frying pan over a medium heat. Add the pork chops and cook for about 6–7 minutes on each side until cooked through. Drain the pork chops and set aside the pan juices. Keep warm.

3 Add the butter to the pan. Add the lemon juice, sugar and tomatoes and cook for 5 minutes until tender. Transfer the chops to 4 warmed serving plates and pour over the pan juices. Serve with the tomato and onion mixture and a green salad.

fresh spaghetti & meatballs

serves four

150 g/5½ oz brown breadcrumbs

150 ml/ 5 fl oz milk

25 g/1 oz butter

25 g/1 oz wholemeal flour

200 ml/7 fl oz beef stock

400 g/14 oz canned
   chopped tomatoes

2 tbsp tomato purée

1 tsp sugar

1 tbsp finely chopped fresh tarragon

1 large onion, chopped

450 g/1 lb minced steak

1 tsp paprika

4 tbsp olive oil

450 g/1 lb fresh spaghetti

salt and pepper

fresh tarragon leaves, to garnish

1 Soak the breadcrumbs in the milk for 30 minutes.

2 Melt half the butter in a pan over a low heat. Add the flour and cook, stirring, for 2 minutes. Stir in the stock and cook for 5 minutes. Add the tomatoes, tomato purée, sugar and tarragon. Season to taste with salt and pepper and cook for 25 minutes.

3 Mix the onion, steak and paprika into the breadcrumbs and season to taste. Shape into 16 meatballs.

4 Heat the oil and remaining butter in a pan over a medium heat. Fry the meatballs until browned. Put in a casserole dish and pour over the sauce. Bake in a preheated oven at 180°C/350°F/Gas Mark 4, for 25 minutes.

5 Bring a large pan of lightly salted water to the boil over a medium heat. Add the pasta and cook until tender, but still firm to the bite.

6 Remove the meatballs from the oven. Pile the pasta on to plates, add the meatballs with their sauce and garnish with fresh tarragon. Serve.

spaghetti bolognese

serves four

1 tbsp olive oil

1 onion, chopped finely

2 garlic cloves, chopped

1 carrot, scraped and chopped

1 celery stick, chopped

50 g/1¾ oz pancetta or streaky
   bacon, diced

350 g/12 oz lean minced beef

400 g/14 oz canned
   chopped tomatoes

2 tsp dried oregano

125 ml/4 fl oz red wine

2 tbsp tomato purée

salt and pepper

350 g/12 oz dried spaghetti

freshly grated Parmesan cheese,
   to serve (optional)

VARIATION

Try adding 25 g/1 oz dried
porcini, soaked for 20 minutes
in 2 tbsp of warm water, to the
bolognese sauce in
step 4, if you wish.

---

1 Heat the oil in a large frying pan over a medium heat. Add the onions and cook for 3 minutes.

2 Add the garlic, carrot, celery and pancetta or bacon and sauté for 3–4 minutes over a fairly hot heat or until just starting to brown.

3 Add the beef and cook over a high heat for a further 3 minutes, or until all of the meat is browned.

4 Stir in the tomatoes, oregano and red wine and bring to the boil over a medium heat. Reduce the heat and simmer for about 45 minutes.

5 Stir in the tomato purée and season with salt and pepper.

6 Bring a large pan of lightly salted water to the boil over a medium heat. Add the pasta and cook for 8–10 minutes, or until tender, but still firm to the bite. Drain thoroughly.

7 Transfer the pasta to a large serving plate and pour over the bolognese sauce. Serve immediately with Parmesan cheese, if you wish.

spaghetti with ricotta cheese sauce

serves four

350 g/12 oz dried spaghetti

3 tbsp butter

2 tbsp chopped fresh
  flat-leaf parsley

1 tbsp pine kernels

salt and pepper

1 fresh flat-leaf parsley sprig,
  to garnish

RICOTTA CHEESE SAUCE

115 g/4 oz freshly ground almonds

115 g/4 oz ricotta cheese

pinch of freshly grated nutmeg

pinch of ground cinnamon

150 ml/5 fl oz crème fraîche

2 tbsp olive oil

125 ml/4 fl oz hot chicken stock

1 Bring a large pan of lightly salted water to the boil over a medium heat. Add the pasta and cook for about 8–10 minutes, or until tender, but still firm to the bite.

2 Drain the pasta, return to the pan and toss with the butter and parsley. Reserve and keep warm.

3 To make the ricotta cheese sauce, mix the ground almonds, ricotta cheese, nutmeg, cinnamon and crème fraîche together in a small pan and stir over a low heat until it forms a thick paste. Gradually stir in the oil. When the oil has been fully incorporated, gradually stir in the stock until smooth. Season with pepper to taste.

4 Transfer the pasta to a large warmed serving dish, pour the sauce over it and toss together well with 2 forks (see Cook's Tip). Sprinkle over the pine kernels, garnish with a parsley sprig and serve immediately.

COOK'S TIP

It is best to use 2 large forks to toss the cooked spaghetti or other long pasta as this ensures that the pasta is thoroughly coated with the sauce. You can also purchase specially designed spaghetti forks, which are available from some cookware departments and large kitchen shops.

spaghetti olio e aglio

serves four

125 ml/4 fl oz olive oil

3 garlic cloves, crushed

450 g/1 lb fresh spaghetti

3 tbsp roughly chopped
   fresh parsley

salt and pepper

COOK'S TIP

Olive oils produced by different
countries, mainly Italy, Spain
and Greece, have their own
characteristic flavours. Some oils
have a rather hot, peppery
taste while others have a quite
mild 'green' flavour.

1 Reserve 1 tablespoon of the oil
and heat the remainder in a pan
over a low heat. Add the garlic and
a pinch of salt and cook, stirring
constantly, until golden brown.
Remove the pan from the heat. Do not
allow the garlic to burn as it will taint
the flavour of the oil. (If it does burn,
you will have to start all over again!)

2 Meanwhile, bring a large pan of
lightly salted water to the boil
over a medium heat. Add the spaghetti
and remaining oil and cook for about
2–3 minutes, or until tender, but still
firm to the bite. Drain the pasta
thoroughly and return to the pan.

3 Add the oil and garlic mixture to
the pasta and toss with 2 forks to
coat thoroughly. Season with pepper to
taste, add the chopped parsley and
toss well to coat again.

4 Transfer the pasta to a warmed
serving dish and serve.

pasta with cheese & broccoli

serves four

300 g/10½ oz dried
   tricolour tagliatelle
225 g/8 oz broccoli, broken into
   small florets
350 g/12 oz mascarpone cheese
125 g/4½ oz blue cheese, chopped
1 tbsp chopped fresh oregano
25 g/1 oz butter
salt and pepper
fresh oregano sprigs, to garnish
freshly grated Parmesan cheese,
   to serve

1 Bring a large pan of lightly salted water to the boil over a medium heat. Add the pasta and cook until tender, but still firm to the bite.

2 Cook the broccoli in a small amount of lightly salted boiling water. Avoid overcooking to retain much of its colour and texture.

3 Melt the mascarpone and blue cheeses together in a small pan over a very low heat. Stir in the chopped oregano and season to taste with salt and pepper.

4 Drain the pasta thoroughly and return to the pan. Add the butter and, using 2 forks, toss the pasta until coated with the butter. Drain the broccoli well and add to the pasta with the sauce, tossing gently to mix.

5 Transfer the pasta to 4 warmed serving plates. Garnish with fresh oregano sprigs and serve immediately with Parmesan cheese.

tagliatelle & garlic sauce

serves four

2 tbsp walnut oil

1 bunch spring onions, sliced

2 garlic cloves, sliced thinly

225 g/8 oz mushrooms, sliced

500 g/1 lb 2 oz fresh green and
 white tagliatelle

225 g/8 oz frozen chopped spinach,
 thawed and drained

125 g/4½ oz full-fat soft cheese
 flavoured with garlic and herbs

4 tbsp single cream

55 g/2 oz chopped, unsalted
 pistachio nuts

2 tbsp shredded fresh basil

salt and pepper

4 fresh basil sprigs, to garnish

Italian bread, to serve

1 Heat the oil in a frying pan over a low heat. Add the spring onions and garlic and fry for 1 minute or until just softened. Add the mushrooms to the pan, stir well, cover and cook gently for 5 minutes or until softened.

2 Bring a large pan of lightly salted water to the boil over a medium heat. Add the pasta and cook for 3–5 minutes, or until just tender, but still firm to the bite. Drain thoroughly and return to the pan.

3 Add the spinach to the mushrooms and heat through for 1–2 minutes. Add the cheese and melt slightly. Stir in the cream and heat without allowing it to boil.

4 Pour the vegetable mixture over the pasta, season to taste with salt and pepper and mix well. Heat gently, stirring, for 2–3 minutes.

5 Transfer the pasta to 4 warmed serving plates and sprinkle over the pistachio nuts and shredded basil. Garnish with a fresh basil sprig and serve with Italian bread.

fettuccine all'alfredo

serves four

25 g/1 oz butter

200 ml/7 fl oz double cream

450 g/1 lb fresh fettuccine

85 g/3 oz freshly grated Parmesan
    cheese, plus extra to serve

pinch of freshly grated nutmeg

salt and pepper

1 fresh flat-leaf parsley sprig,
    to garnish

VARIATION

This classic Roman dish is often
served with the addition of strips
of ham and fresh peas. Add
225 g/8 oz shelled cooked peas
and 175 g/6 oz ham strips with
the Parmesan cheese in step 4.

---

1 Put the butter and 150 ml/5 fl oz
of the cream into a large pan and
bring to the boil over a medium heat.
Reduce the heat, then simmer gently
for about 1½ minutes, or until the
sauce has thickened slightly.

2 Meanwhile, bring a large pan of
lightly salted water to the boil
over a medium heat. Add the pasta
and cook for 2–3 minutes, or until
tender, but still firm to the bite. Drain
the pasta thoroughly, then pour over
the cream sauce.

3 Toss the pasta in the sauce over a
low heat until coated thoroughly.

4 Add the remaining cream, the
Parmesan cheese and nutmeg to
the pasta mixture, then season to taste
with plenty of salt and pepper. Toss
thoroughly to coat the pasta while
gently heating through.

5 Transfer the pasta mixture to a
large, warmed serving dish and
garnish with a parsley sprig. Serve
immediately with extra Parmesan
cheese, if you wish.

italian tomato sauce & pasta

serves two

1 tbsp olive oil

1 small onion, chopped finely

1–2 garlic cloves, crushed

350 g/12 oz tomatoes, peeled and chopped

2 tsp tomato purée

2 tbsp water

300–350 g/10½–12 oz dried pasta shapes

85 g/3 oz lean bacon, derinded and diced

40 g/1½ oz mushrooms, sliced

1 tbsp chopped fresh parsley or 1 tsp chopped fresh coriander

2 tbsp soured cream or natural fromage frais, optional

salt and pepper

COOK'S TIP

Soured cream contains 18–20% fat, so if you are following a low-fat diet you can leave it out of this recipe or substitute a low-fat alternative.

1 Heat the oil in a pan over a low heat. Add the onion and garlic and fry until soft.

2 Add the tomatoes, tomato purée and water. Season to taste with salt and pepper and bring to the boil over a low heat. Cover and simmer gently for 10 minutes.

3 Bring a pan of lightly salted water to the boil over a medium heat. Add the pasta and cook until tender, but still firm to the bite. Drain well and transfer to 2 warmed serving dishes.

4 Heat the bacon in a frying pan over a low heat and cook until the fat runs, then add the mushrooms and cook for 3–4 minutes. Drain off any excess oil.

5 Add the bacon and mushrooms to the tomato mixture, together with the chopped parsley and the soured cream (if using). Heat through and serve immediately with the pasta.

milanese risotto

serves four

2 good pinches of saffron threads
85 g/3 oz butter
1 large onion, chopped finely
1–2 garlic cloves, crushed
350 g/12 oz arborio rice
150 ml/5 fl oz dry white wine
1.2 litres/2 pints boiling
   vegetable stock
85 g/3 oz freshly grated
   Parmesan cheese
salt and pepper

1 Put the saffron into a small bowl, cover with 3–4 tablespoons of almost boiling water and leave to soak while you prepare the risotto.

2 Melt 55 g/2 oz of the butter in a pan over a low heat. Add the onion and garlic and fry until soft but not coloured. Add the rice and cook for 2–3 minutes, or until the grains are coated in oil and starting to colour.

3 Add the wine to the rice and simmer gently, stirring from time to time, until it is all absorbed.

4 Add a ladleful (150 ml/5 fl oz) of the hot stock. Cook, stirring constantly, until the liquid is absorbed before adding more.

5 When all the stock has been absorbed (this should take about 20 minutes), the rice should be tender but not soft and soggy. Add the saffron liquid, Parmesan cheese and remaining butter. Season to taste with salt and pepper and simmer for 2 minutes until piping hot and thoroughly mixed.

6 Cover the pan tightly and leave to stand for 5 minutes off the heat. Give a good stir and serve immediately.

sun-dried risotto

serves six

about 12 sun-dried tomatoes,
   not in oil

2 tbsp olive oil

1 large onion, chopped finely

4–6 garlic cloves, chopped finely

400 g/14 oz arborio or carnaroli rice

1.5 litres/2¾ pints chicken or
   vegetable stock, simmering

115 g/4 oz frozen peas, thawed

2 tbsp chopped fresh
   flat-leaf parsley

115 g/4 oz freshly grated aged
   pecorino cheese

1 tbsp extra virgin olive oil

1 Put the sun-dried tomatoes into a bowl and pour over enough boiling water to cover. Stand for about 30 minutes or until soft and supple. Drain and pat dry with kitchen paper, then shred thinly and reserve.

2 Heat the oil in a frying pan over a medium heat. Add the onion and cook for 2 minutes until starting to soften. Add the garlic and cook for 15 seconds. Add the rice and cook, stirring, for 2 minutes, or until the rice is translucent and coated with oil.

3 Add a ladleful of the hot stock, which will bubble and steam rapidly. Cook gently, stirring constantly, until the liquid is absorbed.

4 Continue adding the stock, about half a ladleful at a time, letting each addition be absorbed by the rice before adding the next.

5 After about 15 minutes, stir in the sun-dried tomatoes. Continue to cook, adding the stock, until the rice is tender, but firm to the bite. Add the peas with the last addition of stock.

6 Remove from the heat and stir in the parsley and half the cheese. Cover, leave to stand for 1 minute, then spoon into 6 dishes. The risotto should have a creamy consistency. Drizzle with oil and sprinkle with the remaining cheese. Serve immediately.

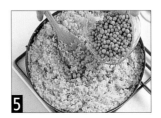

green risotto

serves four

1 onion, chopped

2 tbsp olive oil

225 g/8 oz risotto rice

700 ml/1¼ pints hot vegetable stock

350 g/12 oz mixed green
vegetables, such as asparagus,
fine green beans, mangetout,
courgettes, broccoli florets,
frozen peas

2 tbsp chopped fresh parsley

55 g/2 oz Parmesan
cheese shavings

salt and pepper

COOK'S TIP

For extra texture, stir in
a few toasted pine kernels
or coarsely chopped cashew
nuts at the end of the
cooking time.

1 Put the onion and oil into a large bowl. Cover and cook in the microwave on HIGH for 2 minutes.

2 Add the rice and stir until coated thoroughly in the oil. Pour in about 5 tablespoons of the hot stock. Cook, uncovered, for 2 minutes, until the liquid is absorbed. Pour in another 5 tablespoons of the stock and cook, uncovered, on HIGH for 2 minutes. Repeat once more.

3 Chop or slice the vegetables into even-sized pieces. Stir into the rice with the remaining stock. Cover and cook on HIGH for 8 minutes,

stirring occasionally, until most of the liquid has been absorbed and the rice is just tender.

4 Stir in the chopped parsley and season with salt and pepper. Leave to stand, covered, for 5 minutes. The rice should be tender and creamy.

5 Transfer to a large serving dish and scatter the Parmesan cheese over the risotto before serving.

wild mushroom risotto

serves six

55 g/2 oz dried porcini or
   morel mushrooms

about 500 g/1 lb 2 oz mixed fresh
   wild mushrooms, such as porcini,
   girolles, horse mushrooms and
   chanterelles, halved if large

4 tbsp olive oil

3–4 garlic cloves, chopped finely

4 tbsp unsalted butter

1 onion, chopped finely

350 g/12 oz arborio or carnaroli rice

3 tablespoons dry white vermouth

1.2 litres/2 pints chicken
   stock, simmering

115 g/4 oz freshly grated
   Parmesan cheese

4 tbsp chopped fresh parsley

salt and pepper

6 fresh parsley sprigs, to garnish

crusty bread, to serve

1 Put the mushrooms into a bowl and pour over enough almost boiling water to cover. Leave to soak for 30 minutes, then lift out and pat dry. Strain the soaking liquid through a sieve lined with kitchen paper. Reserve.

2 Trim the fresh wild mushrooms and gently brush clean.

3 Heat 3 tablespoons of the oil in a large frying pan over a low heat. Add the fresh mushrooms and stir-fry for 1–2 minutes. Add the garlic and the soaked mushrooms and cook, stirring frequently, for 2 minutes. Transfer to a plate and reserve.

4 Heat the remaining oil and half the butter in a frying pan over a low heat. Add the onion and cook, stirring occasionally, for about 2 minutes until softened. Add the rice and cook, stirring frequently, for about 2 minutes until translucent and well coated.

5 Add the vermouth. When almost absorbed, add a ladleful (about 225 ml/8 fl oz) of the stock. Cook, stirring constantly, until the liquid is absorbed.

6 Continue adding the stock, about half a ladleful at a time, allowing each addition to be completely absorbed before adding the next. This should take 20–25 minutes. The risotto should have a creamy consistency and the rice should be tender, but still firm to the bite.

7 Add half the reserved mushroom soaking liquid to the risotto and stir in the mushrooms. Season to taste with salt and pepper and add more mushroom liquid, if necessary. Remove the pan from the heat and stir in the remaining butter, the Parmesan cheese and chopped parsley. Transfer the risotto to 6 warmed serving dishes, garnish with parsley sprigs and serve immediately with crusty bread.

pesto rice with garlic bread

serves four

300 g/10½ oz mixed long-grain and
    wild rice
4 fresh basil sprigs, to garnish
tomato and orange salad, to serve
PESTO SAUCE
15 g/½ oz fresh basil sprigs
125 g/4½ oz pine kernels
2 garlic cloves, crushed
6 tbsp olive oil
55 g/2 oz freshly grated
    Parmesan cheese
salt and pepper
GARLIC BREAD
2 small French bread sticks
85 g/3 oz butter or
    margarine, softened
2 garlic cloves, crushed
1 tsp dried mixed herbs

1 Put the rice into a pan and cover
    with water. Bring to the boil over
a medium heat and cook for about
15–20 minutes. Drain and keep warm.

2 To make the pesto sauce, remove
    the basil leaves from the stalks
and finely chop the leaves. Reserve
25 g/1 oz of the pine kernels and finely
chop the remainder. Mix with the

chopped basil and the rest of the sauce
ingredients. Alternatively, put all the
ingredients into a food processor and
process for a few seconds until
smooth. Reserve.

3 To make the garlic bread, slice the
    bread at 2.5 cm/1 inch intervals,
taking care not to slice all the way
through. Mix the butter or margarine
with the garlic and herbs. Season to
taste with salt and pepper. Spread
thickly between each slice.

4 Wrap in tinfoil and bake in a
    preheated oven at 200°C/
400°F/Gas Mark 6, for 10–15 minutes.

5 To serve, toast the reserved pine
    kernels under a preheated
medium grill for 2–3 minutes until
golden. Toss the pesto sauce into the
hot rice and pile into 4 warmed serving
dishes. Sprinkle with toasted pine
kernels and garnish with a few basil
sprigs. Serve with the garlic bread and
a tomato and orange salad.

potato & spinach gnocchi

serves four

300 g/10½ oz floury potatoes,
    peeled and diced
175 g/6 oz fresh spinach leaves
1 egg yolk
1 tsp olive oil
125 g/4½ oz plain flour
salt and pepper
fresh spinach leaves, to garnish
SAUCE
1 tbsp olive oil
2 shallots, chopped
1 garlic clove, crushed
300 ml/10 fl oz passata
2 tsp soft light brown sugar

1 Bring a large pan of water to the boil over a medium heat. Add the potatoes and cook for 10 minutes or until cooked. Drain well, then mash.

2 Blanch the spinach in a little boiling water for 1–2 minutes. Drain and shred the leaves.

3 Transfer the potato to a lightly floured chopping board and make a well in the centre. Add the egg yolk, oil, spinach, salt and pepper and a little of the flour and quickly mix into the potato, adding more flour, until you have a firm dough. Divide the mixture into very small dumplings.

4 Bring a large pan of lightly salted water to the boil over a medium heat. Add the gnocchi, in batches, and cook for about 5 minutes, or until they rise to the surface.

5 To make the sauce, put the oil, shallots, garlic, passata and sugar into a pan and cook over a low heat for 10–15 minutes, or until the sauce is thickened.

6 Drain the gnocchi with a slotted spoon and transfer to 4 warmed serving dishes. Spoon the sauce over the gnocchi and garnish with the fresh spinach leaves. Serve immediately.

spinach & ricotta gnocchi

serves four

1 kg/2 lb 4 oz fresh spinach leaves

350 g/12 oz ricotta cheese

125 g/4½ oz freshly grated
    pecorino cheese

3 eggs, beaten

¼ tsp freshly grated nutmeg

plain flour, to mix

1 tsp olive oil

125 g/4½ oz unsalted butter

25 g/1 oz pine kernels

55 g/2 oz raisins

salt and pepper

1 Wash and drain the spinach well. Cook in a covered pan without any extra liquid for about 4 minutes, until softened, then put into a colander and press well to remove as much liquid as possible. Put the spinach into a blender and process until smooth. Alternatively, rub through a sieve.

2 Mix the spinach purée with the ricotta, half the pecorino cheeses, the eggs and nutmeg. Season to taste with salt and pepper, then mix lightly but thoroughly. Work in enough flour, lightly and quickly, to make the mixture easy to handle.

3 Shape the dough quickly into small oval shapes, and dust lightly with a little flour.

4 Add a dash of oil to a large pan of lightly salted water and bring to the boil over a medium heat. Add the gnocchi carefully and boil for about 2 minutes, or until they rise to the surface. Transfer the gnocchi to an ovenproof dish with a slotted spoon and keep warm.

5 Melt the butter in a frying pan. Add the pine kernels and raisins and fry until the nuts start to brown slightly, but do not allow the butter to burn.

6 Transfer the gnocchi to 4 dishes, pour the mixture over and sprinkle with remaining cheese. Serve.

baked semolina gnocchi

serves four

450 ml/16 fl oz vegetable stock

100 g/3½ oz semolina

1 tbsp fresh thyme, stalks removed

1 egg, beaten

50 g/1¾ oz freshly grated
  Parmesan cheese

50 g/1¾ oz butter

2 garlic cloves, crushed

salt and pepper

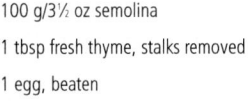

1 Put the stock into a large pan and bring to the boil over a medium heat. Add the semolina in a steady trickle, stirring constantly. Keep stirring for 3–4 minutes, or until the mixture is thick enough to hold a spoon upright. Leave to cool slightly.

2 Add the thyme leaves, egg and half the cheese to the semolina mixture, then season to taste with salt and pepper.

3 Spread the semolina mixture on a board to a thickness of about 8 mm/⅜ inch and leave until it has cooled and set.

4 When the semolina is cold, cut it into 2.5-cm/1-inch squares, reserving any offcuts.

5 Grease a large ovenproof dish, placing the reserved offcuts in the bottom. Arrange the semolina squares on top, then sprinkle with the remaining cheese.

6 Melt the butter in a pan over a low heat. Add the garlic and season with pepper. Pour the mixture over the gnocchi. Bake in a preheated oven at 220°C/425°F/Gas Mark 7, for 15–20 minutes, or until the gnocchi are puffed up and golden. Serve hot.

pan potato cake

serves four

675 g/1½ lb waxy potatoes,
    unpeeled and sliced

1 carrot, diced

225 g/8 oz small broccoli florets

5 tbsp butter

2 tbsp vegetable oil

1 red onion, quartered

2 garlic cloves, crushed

175 g/6 oz firm tofu, drained and
    diced

2 tbsp chopped fresh sage

75 g/2¼ oz mature cheese, grated

1 Cook the sliced potatoes in a large saucepan of boiling water for 10 minutes. Drain thoroughly.

2 Meanwhile, cook the carrot and broccoli florets in a separate pan of boiling water for 5 minutes. Drain with a slotted spoon.

3 Heat the butter and oil in a 23-cm/9-inch frying pan. Add the onion and garlic and fry over a low heat for 2–3 minutes. Add half of the potato slices to the frying pan, covering the base of the pan.

4 Cover the potato slices with the carrot, broccoli and the tofu. Sprinkle with half of the sage and cover with the remaining potato slices. Sprinkle the grated cheese over the top.

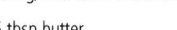

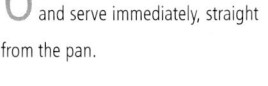

5 Cook over a moderate heat for 8–10 minutes. Then place the pan under a preheated medium grill for 2–3 minutes, or until the cheese melts and browns.

6 Garnish with the remaining sage and serve immediately, straight from the pan.

69

polenta kebabs

serves four

175 g/6 oz instant polenta

700 ml/1¼ pints water

2 tbsp fresh thyme, stalks removed

8 slices Parma ham (about
    75 g/2¾ oz)

1 tbsp olive oil

salt and pepper

fresh green salad, to serve

COOK'S TIP

Try flavouring the polenta with chopped fresh oregano, basil or marjoram instead of the thyme, if you prefer. You should use 1½ tbsp of chopped herbs to every 175 g/6 oz instant polenta.

1 Cook the polenta with the water, stirring occasionally. Alternatively, follow the packet instructions.

2 Add the fresh thyme leaves to the polenta mixture and season to taste with salt and pepper.

3 Spread out the polenta, about 2.5-cm/1-inch thick, on a board. Leave to cool.

4 Cut the polenta into 2.5-cm/1-inch cubes with a sharp knife.

5 Cut the Parma ham slices into 2 pieces lengthways. Wrap the Parma ham around the polenta cubes.

6 Thread the polenta cubes on to presoaked bamboo skewers.

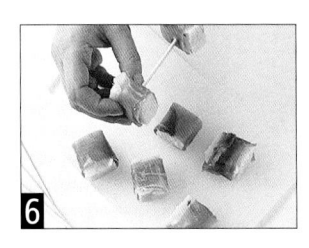

7 Brush the kebabs with a little oil and cook under a preheated hot grill, turning frequently, for 7–8 minutes. Alternatively, barbecue until golden. Transfer to 4 serving plates and serve with a green salad.

mascarpone cheesecake

serves eight

1½ tbsp unsalted butter, plus extra
   for greasing
150 g/5½ oz ginger
   biscuits, crushed
25 g/1 oz stem ginger, chopped
500 g/1 lb 2 oz mascarpone cheese
finely grated rind and juice of
   2 lemons
100 g/3½ oz caster sugar
2 eggs, separated
fruit coulis (see Cook's Tip), to serve

COOK'S TIP

Fruit coulis can be made by
cooking 400 g/14 oz fruit, such
as blueberries, for 5 minutes
with 2 tbsp of water. Sieve the
mixture, then stir in
1 tbsp (or more to taste)
of sifted icing sugar. Leave to
cool before serving.

1 Grease and line the base of a 25-cm/10-inch spring-form cake tin or loose-bottomed tin.

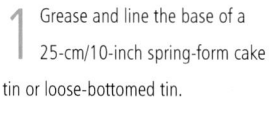

2 Melt the butter in a pan over a low heat and stir in the crushed biscuits and ginger. Use the mixture to line the tin, pressing the mixture about 5 mm/¼ inch up the sides.

3 Beat the cheese, lemon rind and juice, sugar and egg yolks together until quite smooth.

4 Whisk the egg whites in a separate spotlessly clean grease-free bowl until stiff peaks form. Fold into the cheese and lemon mixture.

5 Pour the mixture into the prepared tin and bake in a preheated oven at 180°C/350°F/Gas Mark 4, for 35–45 minutes until just set. Don't worry if it cracks or sinks as this is quite normal.

6 Leave the cheesecake in the tin to cool, then serve with fruit coulis (see Cook's Tip).

tuscan pudding

serves four

1 tbsp butter

75 g/2¾ oz mixed dried fruit

250 g/9 oz ricotta cheese

3 egg yolks

50 g/1¾ oz caster sugar

1 tsp ground cinnamon

finely grated rind of 1 orange, plus
    orange zest to decorate

crème fraîche, to serve

COOK'S TIP

Crème fraîche has a slightly
sour, nutty taste and is very
thick. It is suitable for both
cooking or for serving cold.

1 Grease 4 mini pudding basins or
ramekin dishes with the butter.

2 Put the dried fruit into a bowl and
pour over enough warm water to
cover. Leave to soak for 10 minutes.

3 Beat the ricotta cheese with the
egg yolks in a bowl. Stir in the
caster sugar, ground cinnamon and
orange rind and mix well.

4 Drain the dried fruit in a sieve set
over a bowl. Mix the drained fruit
with the ricotta cheese mixture.

5 Spoon the mixture into the
prepared basins or ramekins.

6 Bake in a preheated oven at
180°C/350°F/Gas Mark 4, for
15 minutes. The tops should be firm to
the touch but not browned.

7 Invert the puddings on to
4 serving plates and decorate
with orange zest. Serve with a
spoonful of crème fraîche, if you wish.

summer puddings

serves six

1 tbsp oil or butter for greasing

6–8 thin slices white bread,
   crusts removed

175 g/6 oz caster sugar

300 ml/10 fl oz water

225 g/8 oz strawberries

500 g/1 lb 2 oz raspberries

175 g/6 oz blackcurrants
   and/or redcurrants

175 g/6 oz blackberries
   or loganberries

single cream, to serve

1 Grease 6 150-ml/5-fl oz moulds with the butter or oil.

2 Line the moulds with the bread, cutting the slices to fit snugly.

3 Put the sugar in a small pan with the water and heat gently, stirring until dissolved. Bring to the boil over a high heat and boil for 2 minutes.

4 Reserve 6 large strawberries for the decoration. Add half the raspberries and the rest of the fruits to the syrup, cutting the strawberries in half if large, and simmer gently for a few minutes, until they are starting to soften but still retain their shape.

5 Spoon the fruits and some of the liquid into moulds. Cover with more slices of bread. Spoon a little juice around the sides of the moulds so the bread is well soaked. Cover with a saucer and a heavy weight, leave to cool, then chill thoroughly in the refrigerator, preferably overnight.

6 Put the remaining raspberries in a food processor and process until smooth. Alternatively, rub through a sieve. Add enough of the liquid from the fruits to give a coating consistency.

7 Invert on to serving plates and spoon the raspberry sauce over. Decorate with the reserved strawberries and serve with cream.

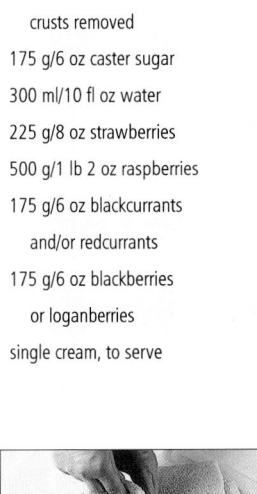

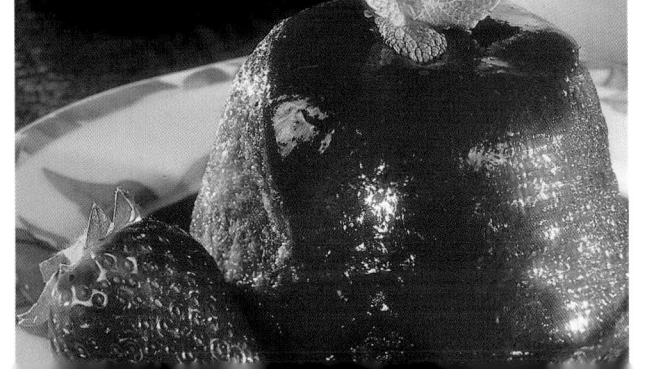

chocolate zabaglione

serves four

4 egg yolks

4 tbsp caster sugar

50 g/1¾ oz dark chocolate

125 ml/4 fl oz Marsala wine

amaretti biscuits, to serve

COOK'S TIP

Make the dessert just before serving as it will separate if left to stand. If it begins to curdle, remove it from the heat immediately and put into a bowl of cold water to stop the cooking. Whisk furiously until the mixture comes together.

1 Put the egg yolks and caster sugar into a large glass bowl and, using an electric whisk, whisk together until the mixture is very pale.

2 Grate the chocolate finely and fold into the egg mixture.

3 Fold the Marsala wine into the chocolate mixture.

4 Put the bowl over a pan of gently simmering water and set the electric whisk on the lowest speed or swap to a balloon whisk. Cook gently, whisking continuously, until the mixture thickens. Take care not to overcook or the mixture will curdle.

5 Spoon the hot mixture into warmed individual glass dishes or coffee cups and serve the zabaglione as soon as possible, while it is warm, light and fluffy accompanied by amaretti biscuits.

This is a Parragon Book
This edition published in 2005

Parragon
Queen Street House
4 Queen Street
Bath BA1 1HE, UK

ISBN: 1-40544-092-9

Printed in China
Photography and text by the Bridgewater Book Company Ltd

NOTE

This book also uses metric and imperial measurements. Follow the same units
of measurement throughout; do not mix metric and imperial.
All spoon measurements are level: teaspoons are assumed to be 5 ml and
tablespoons are assumed to be 15 ml. Unless otherwise stated, milk is assumed
to be full fat milk, eggs and individual vegetables such as potatoes are medium,
and pepper is freshly ground black pepper.

The times given for each recipe are an approximate guide only because the
preparation times may differ according to the techniques used by different
people and the cooking times may vary as a result of the type of oven used.

Recipes using raw or very lightly cooked eggs should be
avoided by infants, the elderly, pregnant women, convalescents and anyone
suffering from an illness.